Portuguese Cooking

Easy Classic Recipes from Portugal

Sarah Spencer

Copyrights

All rights reserved © Sarah Spencer and The Cookbook Publisher. No part of this publication or the information in it may be quoted from or reproduced in any form by means such as printing, scanning, photocopying, or otherwise without prior written permission of the copyright holder.

Disclaimer and Terms of Use

Effort has been made to ensure that the information in this book is accurate and complete. However, the author and the publisher do not warrant the accuracy of the information, text, and graphics contained within the book due to the rapidly changing nature of science, research, known and unknown facts, and internet. The author and the publisher do not hold any responsibility for errors, omissions, or contrary interpretation of the subject matter herein. This book is presented solely for motivational and informational purposes only.

The recipes provided in this book are for informational purposes only and are not intended to provide dietary advice. A medical practitioner should be consulted before making any changes in diet. Additionally, recipe cooking times may require adjustment depending on age and quality of appliances. Readers are strongly urged to take all precautions to ensure ingredients are fully cooked in order to avoid the dangers of foodborne illnesses. The recipes and suggestions provided in this book are solely the opinion of the author. The author and publisher do not take any responsibility for any consequences that may result due to following the instructions provided in this book.

ISBN: 978-1976319082

Printed in the United States

Contents

Introduction 1
Recipes 7
Appetizers & Snacks 7
Salads 15
Soups 25
Poultry 33
Pork, Beef & Lamb 45
Seafood 71
Sides 87
Desserts 97
Recipe Index 109
Image Credits 111
Also by Sarah Spencer 113
Appendix - Cooking Conversion Charts 115

Introduction

Portugal's rich and vibrant culture is undeniably felt in its cuisine. Portuguese dishes are never shy. Each dish proudly presents itself with fresh, robust, and surprising flavors. There is something both comforting and celebratory about Portuguese dishes. Hearty soups and stews warm and nourish. With olive oil, one must be extravagant; with meat, nothing is to be put to waste.

Desserts are divine, their flavors and preparation seeming to resound with good times and happy memories. Portuguese cooking transports us back to days when mothers, grandmothers and aunts stuffed us with pastries sprinkled with magic dust; or when fathers brought home the freshest ocean catch. We remember uncles who pitched in, roasting the suckling pig, while grandpa masterfully prepared a rabbit stew.

And we are taken even farther back in time – to when explorers and adventurers sailed away and came back with incredible tales and things that were all so new then – spices, produce and new methods of cooking.

Along with agreeable weather, Portugal is blessed with rich soil and abundant vegetation. Seafood is bountiful and diverse. A look at just a few iconic dishes offers a glimpse of the many influences on Portuguese cuisine.

Caldo Verde or "Green Soup" is a traditional mainstay at celebrations like weddings and birthdays. It is a broth teeming with greens and olive oil, which unsurprisingly shares many similarities with dishes from the Mediterranean and from Portugal's neighbors in the Iberian Peninsula. The famous custard pastry, *Pasteis de Nata,* was concocted by monks. Egg whites were used to starch the clothing of the religious and it would indeed have been a shame if all those egg yolks were simply thrown away. *Bacalhau*, salted cod coming all the way from Scandinavian waters, is also called "the fish that launched a thousand ships." It was this salt-preserved fish that served as nourishment for sailors before refrigeration was invented. Today, Portugal has perhaps thousands of recipes using *Bacalhau*. *Piri-piri* chicken is one of Portugal's best known dishes, however much pedants insist it is actually African. Nevertheless, this fiery dish is often what foreigners associate with Portuguese cuisine.

And if the Portuguese adopted foods and recipes from far-flung corners of the globe, the exchange was hardly one-sided. The explorers and adventurers who built Portugal's empire also ensured that its own cuisine left its mark in such diverse locations as Brazil, Goa, and Macau.

Some Key Ingredients

Every cuisine has its own favorite ingredients that have shaped the culture's palate and characterize the dishes. Portuguese cuisine is no exception. The ingredients mentioned below are used many times in the recipes in this cookbook.

Bacalhau – Dried, salted cod, which must be rehydrated before use. It is said to have been part of Portuguese cooking for the past thousand years. There are stews, salads, snacks and many more recipes made with *Bacalhau*.

Bay leaf – Also called laurel leaf. This is listed separately from other herbs because it is used in almost all savory dishes to lend aroma.

Cinnamon – The Portuguese use cinnamon liberally in their savory dishes as well as their desserts – as well they should, for it was through their empire-building efforts that this spice became more widely available in Europe. In the past, cinnamon was a mysterious and costly ingredient almost akin to gold, and its great value was one of the factors that pushed Columbus to set sail in search of the Spice Islands.

Chouriço – Delicious spicy sausage. This is Portugal's answer to Spain's *chorizo* and is used in many dishes to lend flavor.

Eggs – Whether boiled, poached, fried or scrambled, eggs are added to almost every possible dish in Portugal. It is said that chickens used to be a kind of currency of the poor, which resulted in the abundance of egg recipes.

Fish and seafood – The Portuguese are one of the biggest consumers of fish in the world. Aside from cod, sardines are also very popular. Many of the dishes capitalize on the freshness and abundance of seafood in the coastal regions. Visitors are often amazed at the different types of fish and seafood available in Portugal.

Garlic – This is ever-present, and in large amounts. Apart from olive oil, this is the one ingredient that the Portuguese can't do without.

Herbs – As already noted, bay leaf is the most popular. Other commonly used herbs include parsley, cilantro and mint.

Lemon – Slices of lemon accompany grilled meat and seafood stews. It blends perfectly with olive oil. Its rind is used to add aroma and flavor to desserts.

Linguiça – A smoked sausage spiced with paprika and used to add flavor to a variety of dishes. It is not as spicy as *chouriço* and contains less fat.

Meat – Pork and beef are cooked all possible ways, and all possible parts of the animal are used. The Portuguese have found ways to make what other cultures discard – such as pig lungs or cow stomach – into mouthwatering fare.

Paprika paste or *Massa de pimentão* – Another popular ingredient, especially in meat dishes. Adds flavor to marinades and sauces.

Olive Oil (*Azeite*) – Vegetables and meats are smothered with olive oil. This is an ingredient that is used generously in almost all recipes. Portugal is said to have been using it since as far back as the Bronze Age. Their olive oil has its own distinct flavor and is of very good quality.

Olives – Black or green, olives are used as a side dish or garnish for many dishes.

Piri-Piri – Made out of herbs and chilies, it is the main ingredient for the famous *piri-piri* chicken. There is still some debate on whether this is truly Portuguese or African; without taking sides on the issue, let's just say that most of its heat comes from an African chili, while "peri-peri" means "pepper-pepper" in Swahili.

Sausages – Portugal has many different types, varying from region to region. Most are made of pork. *Chouriço* is somewhat similar to Spanish *chorizo*. It is described as spicy and garlicky. *Linguiça* is a smoked sausage, spiced with paprika. *Morcela* is blood sausage, also called blood pudding, and very tasty. *Farinheira* is a smoked wheat sausage.

Sea salt – Portugal's salt comes from the sea, and sea salt is preferred in making authentic recipes. Although the recipes here rarely specify sea salt, it is highly recommended. 1 tablespoon sea salt = 1½ teaspoons table salt.

Spices – Aside from *piri-piri* and cinnamon, some other well-loved spices are chili, cumin and paprika.

Vegetables and legumes – Kale is used in large amounts in dishes such as *Caldo Verde*. Potatoes, cabbage, tomatoes, carrots and beans are often served as side dishes.

Vinegar – White wine vinegar is a common condiment found on tables in restaurants, along with olive oil. It is also used for marinades and sauces.

Wine – The Portuguese have a variety of good red and white wines. Used in marinades and even as the main liquid in stews, wine always accompanies a meal. *Vinho verde* is a crisp white wine, not green as its name might suggest. Port is both aperitif and dessert. It is also added to desserts to enhance flavor.

Methods & Equipment

You'll find recipes here that call for grilling, roasting, boiling, braising, baking and frying. The Portuguese have developed a unique cooking style of braising followed by frying. Another particular process that one has to master in making many Portuguese dishes is the method of rehydrating *bacalhau* (in recipe on p23). Also, many swear that the Portuguese method of cooking octopus (p91) gives the most tender and tasty result. *Cataplana* dishes are unique as they require the use of a special pan of the same name. Cooking in a *cataplana* is like stewing, steaming and pressure-cooking all at the same time.

Anyone wanting to try out Portuguese cooking will most likely already have all the necessary tools in the kitchen. There are just a few additional items that can make your cooking less difficult.

Cataplana – A clam-shaped cooking pan. The copper lining makes heat distribution more efficient, and the clamps on the sides help seal in the heat, making it function like a pressure cooker. The food can be also flipped over easily. Most often used for stew recipes with clams and other seafood.

Pressure cooker – This will help cook large pieces of meat more quickly and is also good for cooking octopus Portuguese-style.

Spice grinder – The same thing as a coffee grinder, but to be used exclusively for spices.

Large pots – For rustic, peasant-style recipes requiring large cuts.

Grill – Portuguese meat and seafood recipes are often grilled. Although grilling can also be done in a broiler, the results are a little different.

Mortar and pestle – This is useful for pounding small amounts of herbs and spices to make pastes. It's much easier to clean than a food processor.

Kitchen thermometer – This will help remove the guesswork in roasting and frying dishes.

Traditional recipes have mostly been passed down by mothers to daughters, with no measurements. The Portuguese are an innovative and creative people, and their recipes and methods vary from family to family and from region to region. What one family may consider authentic may seem foreign to another.

With that in mind, the recipes in this cookbook do not claim to be authentic. They are here to give you at least a glimpse of Portugal's gastronomy, to let you taste the flavors dear to its people and to feel its rustic charms. In following the recipes, it is hoped that you will experience the passion and simplicity of Portuguese cooking.

Something as simple as using real Portuguese olive oil, sea salt, coarse-ground pepper and only the freshest ingredients will help you understand why Portuguese food is considered some of the best in the world.

Recipes

Appetizers & Snacks

Clams in Lemon & Garlic (*Ameijoas à Bulhão Pato*)

Serves: 4
Preparation Time: 10 minutes with at least 20 minutes soaking time
Cooking Time: 15 minutes

Ingredients

2¼ pounds clams
½ cup olive oil
4 cloves garlic
1 cup parsley, chopped
¾ cup cilantro, chopped
2 tablespoons lemon juice
Salt and pepper, to taste

Directions

1. Soak the clams in water for 20 minutes to 2 hours. Rinse well and drain.
2. Heat the oil in a skillet over medium heat and sauté the garlic until slightly browned (about 2 minutes).
3. Add the clams and the rest of the ingredients. Cook until clams are done or until they open (about 10 minutes). Discard any unopened clams.

Nutrition (per serving)

Calories 327
Carbs 28.5 g
Fat 24 g
Protein 1.5 g
Sodium 944 mg

Stone-Baked Bread (*Bolo do Caco*)

Serves: 5–10
Preparation Time: 30 minutes plus 1 hour waiting time
Cooking Time: 16–20 minutes

Ingredients
6 teaspoons bakers' yeast
3¼ cups flour, plus extra for dusting
½ tablespoon salt
2 cups warm water, divided

Directions
1. Dissolve the yeast in ½ cup of the water. Leave for about 5–10 minutes or until yeast is activated and water turns frothy.
2. In a bowl, sift in the flour and salt.
3. Add a cup of the water-and-yeast mixture.
4. Mix together with your hands. Add the rest of the water gradually to get a sticky dough, sprinkling your hands now and then with flour so it doesn't stick to your hands.
5. Knead until well blended.

6. Sprinkle the surface of the dough with a little bit of flour and cover the bowl with a towel.
7. Let the dough rise for 1 hour.
8. Gather the dough and place on a floured surface.
9. Divide into pieces about the size of walnuts or, if you want them larger, the size of tennis balls.
10. Roll and flatten to about ½-inch-thick rounds (or 1-inch, if you want bigger buns).
11. Cook on a grill or in a heavy-bottomed skillet over medium low heat (about 8–10 minutes on both sides).
12. Usually served filled with garlic butter and as a side for stews and steak.

Nutrition (per serving)
Calories 142
Carbs 31.2 g
Fat 0 g
Protein 4.4 g
Sodium 120 mg

Salted Lupini Beans (*Tremoços*)

Serves: 4–8
Preparation Time: 15 minutes plus at least 6 days soaking
Cooking Time: 2 hours

Ingredients
½ pound dried lupini beans
Water for soaking
Salt
Olive oil (optional)

Directions
1. Remove any sand or pebbles from the beans. They should also be blemish-free.
2. Rinse beans well and drain.
3. Place in a large pot and add water to cover (by about 2 inches).
4. Let soak overnight (8–24 hours).
5. Drain. Rinse well and add water again to cover.
6. Place over heat and bring to a boil. Simmer gently for 2 hours.
7. Drain and rinse.
8. Soak again in fresh water, draining and replacing the water 3–4 times a day, for 6–14 days. You may or may not refrigerate the beans during this period.
9. Taste the beans for bitterness on about the 6th day. The necessary number of days of soaking will vary.
10. Once the beans are no longer bitter, add salt to the soaking water (about 1 teaspoon to 1 tablespoon salt for every 4 cups of water).
11. Let soak in salted water for 3 hours, to develop flavor, before serving. Add more water to reduce saltiness, or more salt if needed. Keep refrigerated in an airtight container. Will keep for about 2 weeks.
12. Drain desired amount to serve and drizzle with olive oil.

Nutrition (per serving)
Calories 99
Carbs 8.2 g
Fat 2.4 g
Protein 13 g
Sodium 3 mg

Shrimp Croquettes (*Rissóis de Camarão*)

Serves: 8
Preparation Time: 30 minutes
Cooking Time: 40–50 minutes

Ingredients
2 eggs, beaten
1½ cups breadcrumbs
Vegetable oil for frying
Lemon wedges (optional)

For dough
1 cup water
1 cup milk
2 tablespoons butter or margarine
Salt, to taste
2¼ cups all-purpose flour

For filling
2 tablespoons butter or margarine
1 small onion, chopped

1 cup milk, divided
1 tablespoon parsley, chopped
1 teaspoon nutmeg
Salt and pepper, to taste
½ tablespoon all-purpose flour
1 heaping cup shelled shrimp, chopped

Directions
1. Set aside the beaten eggs and breadcrumbs in separate bowls.
2. Prepare the dough and filling (see steps below).
3. Roll the dough out thinly and cut into circles using a glass.
4. Place about 1 teaspoon of filling at the center of the dough.
5. Fold one side over and press the edges to seal.
6. Dip into beaten eggs and then breadcrumbs to coat.
7. Heat the oil, about 2 inches deep, over high heat.
8. Deep fry the rissois until golden brown (about 3 minutes).
9. Drain over paper towels.
10. Serve with lemon wedges (optional).

For dough
11. Heat water, salt and margarine in a saucepan. Bring to a boil.
12. Reduce heat and add flour. Mix continuously with a wooden spoon until mixture separates from sides of pan and forms into a ball.
13. Remove from heat and place on a lightly floured surface. Let cool.
14. Knead until smooth. Set aside.

For filling
15. Dissolve the flour in about ¼ cup of milk. Set aside.
16. Melt the butter or margarine in a skillet over medium heat.
17. Add onion and sauté until browned (about 8–10 minutes).
18. Reduce heat and stir in milk, flour mixture, parsley, nutmeg, salt and pepper.
19. Cook until mixture thickens.
20. Stir in chopped shrimp and cook until heated through (about 1 minute).
21. Remove from heat and let cool.

Nutrition (per serving)
Calories 181
Carbs 17.7 g
Fat 8.4 g
Protein 8.3 g
Sodium 303 mg

Salads

Portuguese Salad

Serves: 4
Preparation Time: 15 minutes
Cooking Time: 0 minutes

Ingredients
1 medium head iceberg/crisphead lettuce, washed, dried and torn into pieces
4 medium tomatoes, sliced
1 medium carrot, shredded
1 small cucumber, sliced
1 small green bell pepper, seeded and sliced thinly
1 small onion, sliced into rings
½ cup pitted olives (black or green)
Lemon wedges, to serve
Fresh parsley, chopped, for garnish

Dressing
2 tablespoons olive oil
2 tablespoons balsamic or red wine vinegar
Salt and pepper, to taste

Directions
1. Whisk the dressing ingredients together in a small bowl and set aside.
2. Arrange the lettuce on a serving dish and top with the tomatoes, carrot, cucumber, green bell pepper, onion and olives.
3. Drizzle with the dressing.
4. Serve with lemon wedges.

Nutrition (per serving)
Calories 141
Carbs 16.1g
Fat 8.6 g
Protein 3 g
Sodium 260 mg

Portuguese Potato Salad

Serves: 6–8
Preparation Time: 20 minutes
Cooking Time: 15–20 minutes

Ingredients
6 medium potatoes, scrubbed and washed
½ teaspoon salt
1 cup peas (frozen or canned, drained)
1 medium carrot, diced
½ small onion, minced finely
¼ cup celery, chopped
2 tablespoons minced parsley

For dressing
1 tablespoon olive oil
½ tablespoon red or white wine vinegar
½ teaspoon honey, or to taste
½ teaspoon garlic powder
½ teaspoon paprika
1 cup mayonnaise
Salt and pepper, to taste

Directions
1. Prepare the dressing by mixing the ingredients together well. Adjust flavor with seasonings, as needed. Cover and refrigerate until ready for use.
2. Potatoes may or may not be peeled. Cut into 1-inch thick pieces.
3. Place in a pot and add water to cover. Bring to a boil.
4. Add salt and simmer 5 minutes, then add carrots.
5. Continue simmering until potatoes are done (about 5 minutes). Don't overcook, or potatoes will be mushy.
6. Add peas and cook to heat through (about 1 minute).
7. Remove from heat and drain. Let cool.
8. Add onions, celery, parsley and dressing.
9. Mix well, but without mashing the potatoes.
10. May be served chilled or at room temperature.

Nutrition (per serving)
Calories 300
Carbs 23.9 g
Fat 21.8 g
Protein 3.6 g
Sodium 243 mg

Bacalhau Salad (Salada de Bacalhau)

Serves: 4
Preparation Time: 20 minutes plus 24–48 hours soaking time
Cooking Time: 5–10 minutes

Ingredients
1 pound *bacalhau* (salted cod)
2 tablespoons olive oil
1 tablespoon mayonnaise
3 cloves garlic, crushed
1 small onion, thinly sliced
1 15-ounce can chickpeas, drained and rinsed
½ cup black olives, chopped
Chopped leaf parsley, to garnish

Directions
To rehydrate bacalhau
1. Soak the bacalhau in water. Cover and refrigerate. Change the water about 3 times in 24 to 48 hours (length of soaking depends on desired saltiness). Drain.

To prepare the salad
2. Boil the bacalhau in water for about 5 to 10 minutes. Drain and let cool.
3. Shred or tear the fish into flakes.
4. Combine the olive oil, mayonnaise, and garlic in a serving bowl.
5. Toss in the onion, chickpeas, olives and the shredded bacalhau.
6. Garnish with parsley.

Nutrition (per serving)
Calories 222
Carbs 27.2 g
Fat 7.4 g
Protein 12.8 g
Sodium 399 mg

Octopus Salad (*Salada de Polvo*)

Serves: 2–4
Preparation Time: 15 minutes plus 15 minutes waiting time
Cooking Time: 0 minutes

Ingredients
1 4-ounce can octopus in garlic oil, or about 1 cup cooked octopus in oil
1 clove garlic, grated
¼ cup red onion, diced
2 small tomatoes, finely diced
½ cup black olives
1 tablespoon fresh basil, chopped
½ cup cilantro, chopped
1 green onion, chopped
2 tablespoons white wine or white balsamic vinegar
1 tablespoon extra-virgin olive oil
Salt and pepper, to taste

Directions
1. Drain the oil from the octopus and cut into bite-size pieces.
2. Mix together with the rest of the ingredients.
3. Let sit for 15 minutes to allow flavors to meld.
4. Serve.

Nutrition (per serving)
Calories 78
Carbs 4.3 g
Fat 5.1 g
Protein 4.5 g
Sodium 127 mg

Tomato Salad (*Salada de Tomate*)

Serves: 2–4
Preparation Time: 15 minutes plus 15 minutes waiting time
Cooking Time: 0 minutes

Ingredients
4 medium tomatoes, chopped
1 red onion, finely chopped
1 tablespoon fresh basil, chopped
1 tablespoon cilantro, chopped
1–2 tablespoons red wine vinegar
¼ teaspoon sugar (optional)
½ tablespoon extra-virgin olive oil
Salt, to taste

Directions
1. If they have been refrigerated, let the tomatoes sit for a few minutes to bring them to room temperature.
2. Combine the rest of the ingredients in a separate bowl.
3. Combine with tomatoes, mixing gently.
4. Let sit for 15 minutes for flavors to meld.
5. Serve.

Nutrition (per serving)
Calories 39
Carbs 5.5 g
Fat 2 g
Protein 0.8 g
Sodium 80 mg

Soups

Portuguese Green Soup (*Caldo Verde*)

Serves: 6
Preparation Time: 10 minutes
Cooking Time: 35 minutes

Ingredients
1–2 tablespoons olive oil
1 onion, chopped
3 cloves garlic, minced
6 potatoes, peeled and sliced
4 cups chicken or vegetable stock
2–3 pieces *linguiça*
6 cups kale, julienned
1 stalk celery, chopped (optional)
Salt and pepper, to taste

Directions
1. Heat the oil in a saucepan or pot over medium heat.
2. Add the onion and garlic and sauté until fragrant (about 3 minutes).
3. Stir in the potatoes and cook to sear slightly (about 3 minutes).
4. Pour in the stock and bring to a boil.
5. Add the linguiça. (Or, to reduce fat content of the soup, slice the linguiça thinly and cook in a separate skillet. Drain off fat and add to soup towards the end of cooking, with the kale.)
6. Boil until potatoes are mushy (about 20 minutes). Turn off heat.
7. Remove the sausage and place on a chopping board. Slice thinly and set aside.
8. Using an immersion blender, puree the potatoes in the broth.
9. Bring back to a boil and then reduce to a simmer.
10. Add the sliced linguiça, celery (optional), kale, salt and pepper.
11. Cook until kale wilts and darkens in color (about 5 minutes).
12. Adjust flavor with salt and pepper, if needed.
13. Serve. Goes well with Broa (Portuguese corn bread, p105).

Nutrition (per serving)
Calories 402
Carbs 45.2 g
Fat 20.2 g
Protein 11.7 g
Sodium 1252 mg

Cabbage & Bean Soup (Sopa de Couve Repolho com Feijão Branco)

Serves: 6–8
Preparation Time: 15 minutes
Cooking Time: 35–45 minutes

Ingredients
6 cups water or chicken stock
1 pound *chouriço*
4 potatoes, peeled and cubed
1 small cabbage, sliced
1 can cooked white kidney beans, drained
Salt and pepper, to taste

Directions
1. Fill a medium size saucepan or pot with the water or chicken stock and bring to a boil.
2. Season with salt and pepper.
3. Add the chouriço and potatoes. Boil until potatoes are mushy (about 20 minutes). Turn off heat.
4. Remove the sausage, slice thinly and set aside.
5. Using an immersion blender, puree the potatoes in the broth.
6. Bring back to a boil and then reduce to a simmer.
7. Add the cabbage. Cook until tender and translucent (about 5 minutes).
8. Add the sliced chouriço and beans and cook to heat through.

Nutrition (per serving)
Calories 365
Carbs 25 g
Fat 22 g
Protein 17.6 g
Sodium 807 mg

Kale Soup (Sopa de Couves)

Serves: 12
Preparation Time: 20 minutes
Cooking Time: 45 minutes

Ingredients
2 16-ounce cans butter beans (lima beans), rinsed and drained, divided
8 cups water
4 cups beef stock
1 medium onion, chopped
4 cloves garlic, chopped
1 bay leaf
½ pound linguica or *chouriço*
1 cup rutabaga, peeled and cut into 1-inch cubes
8–10 cups kale, ribs and stems removed, torn into 1-inch pieces
1 carrot, peeled and diced
6 medium potatoes, peeled and diced
⅓ cup olive oil
¼ cup elbow macaroni
Salt and pepper to taste

Directions

1. Take 1 cup of the beans and mash. Pass through a sieve to remove skin. Set mashed beans aside.
2. Heat the water and stock in a pot and bring to a boil.
3. Add the onion, garlic, bay leaf, rutabaga and chouriço. Let simmer for 20 minutes.
4. Remove the sausage and place on a chopping board. Slice thinly and set aside.
5. Add the carrot, potatoes, kale and olive oil. Cook for 5 minutes.
6. Add the macaroni and cook for 10 minutes.
7. Add the beans and sliced chouriço. Season with salt and pepper.
8. Cook until vegetables and macaroni are done (about 3–5 minutes).
9. Remove bay leaf before serving.

Nutrition (per serving)

Calories 443
Carbs 49.4 g
Fat 20.7 g
Protein 18.6 g
Sodium 946 mg

Stone Soup (*Sopa de Piedra*)

Serves: 8–10
Preparation Time: 15 minutes
Cooking Time: 1 hour 25 minutes

Ingredients
2 tablespoons olive oil
2 leeks, chopped, cleaned, dark green part removed, and sliced
1 small onion, chopped
4 cloves garlic, minced
1 pound *linguiça*
1 cup ham, cut into ½-inch cubes
8 cups chicken stock
2 large carrots, diced
3 medium potatoes, peeled and diced
4 small turnips, peeled and diced
1 small Savoy cabbage, coarsely chopped
1 bay leaf
1 15-ounce can kidney beans, rinsed and drained
1 14½-ounce can diced tomatoes
½ cup fresh parsley

Directions

1. Heat the oil in a pot or saucepan over medium heat.
2. Sauté the onions and leeks until tender (about 10 minutes).
3. Add the garlic and cook until fragrant (about 1 minute).
4. Add the ham and linguiça and cook, with stirring, to sear slightly (about 2 minutes).
5. Stir in the stock, carrots, potatoes, turnips, cabbage and bay leaf.
6. Bring to a boil.
7. Let simmer for 45 minutes. Remove the liguiça, slice and set aside.
8. Add the tomatoes and kidney beans. Simmer for 10 minutes.
9. Add the macaroni and cook until al dente (about 10 minutes).
10. Add the parsley and sliced linguiça. Season with salt and pepper to taste.
11. Remove the bay leaf and serve.

Nutrition (per serving)

Calories 394
Carbs 44.2 g
Fat 14.3 g
Protein 23.2 g
Sodium 1172 mg

Poultry

Garlic Chicken (*Frango Com Alho*)

Serves: 4
Preparation Time: 5 minutes plus 8 hours marinating time
Cooking Time: 30 minutes

Ingredients
8 skinless chicken thighs (you could also use breasts or legs if preferred)
¼ cup olive oil
8 cloves garlic, smashed
1½ teaspoons dried thyme
2 bay leaves
½ cup fortified wine (like sherry, marsala or port)
½ cup chicken broth
1-2 teaspoons Spanish smoked paprika
Salt

Freshly ground black pepper
Fresh parsley, chopped, for garnish

Directions
1. Coat the chicken evenly with smoked paprika. Refrigerate for 8 hours to overnight.
2. Heat oil in a large skillet over medium heat.
3. Sear the chicken until browned but not cooked through (about 5 minutes).
4. Add the smashed garlic and cook until fragrant and slightly browned. Season with salt and pepper to taste.
5. Add the rest of the ingredients except for the parsley.
6. Bring to a boil.
7. Let simmer until sauce is reduced and chicken is done (about 20 minutes).
8. Remove the bay leaves and sprinkle the parsley before serving.

Nutrition (per serving)
Calories 290
Carbs 11 g
Fat 8 g
Protein 28 g
Sodium 368 mg

Duck Rice (Arroz de Pato)

Serves: 4
Preparation Time: 30 minutes
Cooking Time: 1 hour 40 minutes

Ingredients
1 pound duck (about ½ duck)
6 cups water
4 cloves garlic
1 sprig cilantro
1 cube chicken stock
Salt and pepper, to taste
1 egg yolk, beaten
Black or green olives, for garnish (optional)

For seasoning
1 bay leaf
¼ teaspoon nutmeg
½ teaspoon freshly ground pepper
1 tablespoon lemon juice
3 cloves garlic, minced

For rice
½ tablespoon of duck fat or olive oil
1 medium onion, finely chopped or sliced
2 cloves garlic, minced
Dash of salt
2 cups uncooked rice
4 cups duck broth

For duck sauce
1 tablespoon duck fat or olive oil
½ cup *chouriço*, sliced thinly
2 cups shredded duck, seasoned
¼ cup white wine
2 cups duck broth, divided (chicken can be used)
1 tablespoon cornstarch

Directions
1. Place the duck in a pot and add the water (should be enough to cover; add more water if needed).
2. Add the garlic, cilantro, salt and pepper.
3. Bring to a boil and simmer until duck is done (about 40 minutes).
4. Remove the duck and reserve the broth.
5. Remove the duck skin and shred the flesh with a fork.
6. Coat the shredded duck meat well with the seasoning. Set aside.
7. Skim off the duck fat from broth or refrigerate the broth overnight and collect the hardened duck fat on the surface.
8. In a heavy-bottomed saucepan, heat the duck fat or olive oil over medium heat.
9. Sauté the garlic with a dash of salt until fragrant.
10. Add the rice and sauté for about 2 minutes.
11. Stir into the broth and cover. Let cook until the rice is tender and has absorbed the broth (about 15 to 20 minutes). Reduce heat before the broth dries out completely to avoid burning the rice. Remove from heat and set aside.
12. Preheat oven to 375°F.
13. To prepare the duck sauce, first mix about ¼ cup of the broth with the cornstarch to make a slurry. Set aside.
14. Heat the duck fat or oil in a skillet over medium heat.
15. Sauté the onion and sliced chouriço until browned (about 10 minutes).
16. Add the shredded duck and wine. Let boil for a few seconds so the alcohol evaporates.

17. Add the broth and bring to a boil.
18. Stir the slurry a bit and add to the boiling duck-broth mixture.
19. Simmer until thickened (about 3 minutes). Remove from heat.
20. Fluff the cooked rice with a fork and layer with duck sauce in a baking dish.
21. Brush top with egg yolk and bake until surface looks brown and slightly crisp (about 15 to 30 minutes).
22. Serve garnished with olives, if desired.

Nutrition (per serving)
Calories 519
Carbs 49.3 g
Fat 17.8 g
Protein 35.2 g
Sodium 1245 mg

Chicken Barbecue (*Frango No Churrasco*)

Serves: 4–8
Preparation Time: 15 minutes plus 15 minutes marinating time
Cooking Time: 15–20 minutes

Ingredients
1 whole chicken (about 3½ pounds), butterflied and cut into 4 to 8 pieces
2 cloves garlic, crushed
1 tablespoon olive oil
1 tablespoon paprika
1 teaspoon oregano
1 teaspoon dried basil
2 tablespoons paprika sauce or *massa de pimentão* (store-bought or homemade, check below)
1 tablespoon Tabasco sauce or red pepper flakes, or to taste
1 tablespoon lemon juice
Salt and pepper to taste

For basting sauce (optional)
2 tablespoons olive oil
1 tablespoon lemon juice

1 teaspoon hot sauce (like Tabasco or sriracha)
1 bay leaf
Salt and pepper, to taste

Massa de pimentão or paprika sauce
4 red bell peppers, washed and seeded
At least 1 cup refined or sea salt
3 cloves garlic
¼ cup olive oil

Directions
For the chicken
1. Wipe the chicken dry with paper towels.
2. Combine the other ingredients and rub evenly over the chicken pieces.
3. Let the chicken pieces marinate while preheating the oven (about 15 minutes).
4. Preheat oven to 400°F or grill to medium heat. Grate should be lightly oiled. Place a pan of water below the oven grill rack to catch the drippings.
5. Grill the chicken, turning and brushing with basting sauce frequently, until done (about 15 to 20 minutes).
6. Serve hot with rice, fries or a salad.

For basting sauce
7. Combine all ingredients and brush over chicken while grilling.

For paprika sauce
8. Cut the bell pepper into strips.
9. Place in a bowl and cover with as much salt as possible.
10. Let sit overnight.
11. Preheat oven to 250°F.
12. Wash the bell peppers and pat dry.
13. Place on a baking tray, skin up, and bake until skin is loose enough to remove easily. It will begin to blister and turn brown or black (about 2 hours).
14. Let cool a bit, then remove skin.
15. Puree with garlic and olive oil in a blender or food processor to a smooth paste.
16. Will keep for two to three weeks, refrigerated, in an airtight container. Makes about 1 cup.

Nutrition (per serving)
Calories 523
Carbs 1 g
Fat 29 g
Protein 60.7 g
Sodium 270 mg

Eggs with Peas & *Linguiça*

Serves: 4
Preparation Time: 10 minutes
Cooking Time: 25–35 minutes

Ingredients
1 tablespoon olive oil
1 small onion, chopped
2 cloves garlic, minced
1 *linguiça* sausage (about 3.5 ounces), sliced thinly
½ cup red or white wine
4 tomatoes, chopped
3 cups frozen peas
1 teaspoon paprika
1 bay leaf
¼ teaspoon nutmeg
Salt and pepper, to taste
4 large eggs
Cilantro or parsley, chopped, for garnish

Directions
1. Heat the oil in a pan over medium heat.
2. Sauté the onion and garlic until fragrant (about 2 minutes).
3. Add the sausage and cook until brown and crisp.
4. Add in the wine to deglaze, cooking while scraping the browned bits off the bottom of the pan.
5. Add the tomatoes, peas, paprika, bay leaf, nutmeg, salt and pepper.
6. Reduce the heat to medium low and cover. Let simmer until peas are done (about 10 to 15 minutes).
7. Form four 'wells' in the stewed peas for the eggs to be dropped in. Do this carefully so that the yolks don't break.
8. Replace the lid and let cook for 7 to 10 minutes, depending on desired doneness of the eggs.
9. Season with salt and pepper.
10. Sprinkle with cilantro or parsley.
11. Serve hot with bread (like Broa in Sides category p105 or Bolo de Caco in Appetizers & Snacks p11).

Nutrition (per serving)
Calories 290
Carbs 21.6 g
Fat 12.9 g
Protein 17.2 g
Sodium 505 mg

Piri-Piri Chicken

Serves: 4–8
Preparation Time: 20 minutes plus 4 hours marinating time
Cooking Time: 30–40 minutes

Ingredients
1 whole chicken (about 3½ pounds), butterflied
Vegetable or olive oil for brushing
Extra *piri-piri* sauce, store-bought or homemade (recipe below), for dipping

For marinade
2 tablespoons olive oil
1 tablespoon lemon juice
½ cup *piri-piri* sauce
2 tablespoons white wine
Salt and pepper, to taste
1 teaspoon sweet paprika
2 cloves garlic, minced
1 shallot, minced
1 tablespoon ginger, peeled and grated
2 bay leaves

Piri-piri sauce

6 tablespoons lemon juice
1 tablespoon red wine or cider vinegar
1 teaspoon salt
1 cup vegetable or olive oil
¼ cup garlic powder
2 tablespoons paprika
1 tablespoon cayenne pepper
⅓ cup birds eye chilies, stemmed and sliced

Directions
For chicken
1. Combine all marinade ingredients. Place in re-sealable bag such as a Ziplock with chicken.
2. Marinate for 4 to 24 hours, refrigerated, turning frequently.
3. Preheat oven to 400°F or grill to medium heat. Grate should be lightly oiled. Place a pan of water below the oven grill rack to catch the drippings.
4. Grill the chicken, skin-side down, covered, for 10 minutes.
5. Turn over and brush with oil. Continue grilling until well-browned, turning and brushing often (about 30 to 40 minutes).
6. Serve with piri-piri sauce for dipping.

For *piri-piri* sauce
7. Mix the lemon juice, vinegar and salt until the salt is dissolved.
8. Pour into a blender with the other ingredients.
9. Blend until smooth.
10. Let flavors meld for at least 1 hour (1 week optimum) before using.
11. Keeps for 1 month, refrigerated, in an airtight container.

Nutrition (per serving)
Calories 537
Carbs 1.2 g
Fat 30.3 g
Protein 60.7 g
Sodium 258 mg

Pork, Beef & Lamb

Hearty Meat Sandwich with Beer Sauce (*Francesinha*)

Serves: 1
Preparation Time: 20 minutes
Cooking Time: 15–20 minutes

Ingredients
2 thick slices of white bread (about ¾ inch thick)
2 slices smoked ham
8 slices cheese
1 grilled *linguiça* or *chouriço*, sliced thinly
1 fried or roasted slice of beef steak
1 egg, fried or poached (optional)
Salt and pepper, to taste

For sauce
1 can beer
1 cube chicken stock

2 tablespoons tomato paste
¼ cup port, whisky or brandy (or combination thereof)
¼ cup skim milk
2 tablespoons water
1 tablespoon cornstarch
1 bay leaf
Piri-piri sauce (look in Piri-Piri Chicken recipe p47) or chili flakes, to taste

Directions
For sauce
1. Combine the cornstarch and water to make a slurry.
2. In a blender or saucepan, add the slurry and all the sauce ingredients except the bay leaf and piri-piri sauce. Pulse until smooth in blender, or use an immersion blender.
3. Add the bay leaf.
4. While stirring constantly, heat over medium heat until mixture boils. Reduce heat or remove from heat, as needed. Sauce should be free-flowing and not too thick.
5. Remove bay leaf and add piri-piri sauce according to taste.

To assemble the sandwich
6. Set aside 5 slices of cheese.
7. Assemble the sandwich with the fillings, layering the ham, sausage, beef and cheese between the two slices of bread.
8. Drape 1 slice of cheese over each of the sides of the sandwich and place the last piece on top.
9. Top with the egg, if desired. Season with salt and pepper.
10. Grill the sandwich just so the cheese melts and clings to the sandwich (about 5 to 8 minutes). This step can be skipped if the sauce is hot enough to melt the cheese.
11. Pour the hot sauce over the sandwich.
12. Popularly served with French fries and draft beer.

Nutrition (per serving)
Calories 1249
Carbs 68.1 g
Fat 50.4 g
Protein 83.6 g
Sodium 3885 mg

Portuguese Cozido (*Cozido à Portuguesa*)

Serves: 6–8
Preparation Time: 20 minutes
Cooking Time: 1 hour

Ingredients
1 pound beef (large cut for stews like chuck, chuck shoulder or pot roast)
1 pound pork ribs
1 pound pork hock or tail

1 pound chicken breast or thigh
1 piece *morcela* (blood sausage or pudding)
1 piece *chouriço* or *linguiça*
1 piece *farinheira* (flour sausage)
2 large carrots, peeled and cut into large chunks
4 large potatoes, peeled and quartered
3 turnips, peeled and quartered
1 head green cabbage, leaves broken off from stalk
1 pound kale, removed from stalk and rinsed
3 cups uncooked rice
Salt, to taste

Directions
1. Prick the sausages with a fork or skewer and set aside (to be cooked after the other meats).
2. Season the beef, pork and chicken with salt.
3. Boil water (enough for meat pieces to be completely submerged) in a large pot. The pork may be boiled in a separate pot to minimize greasiness.
4. Cook the meats at a low boil. Cooking time will vary for each type of meat, and will also depend on the cut and the desired degree of doneness. Add the chicken towards the end, when the other meats are nearly done. The whole cooking process will take at least 1 hour.
5. Place the vegetables in the boiling water before cooking the sausages. Again, cooking time will vary, ranging from 2 to 10 minutes, depending on the type and cut. The kale should be added last and fished out as soon as the leaves wilt.
6. Scoop out 6 cups of the broth and add to the rice in a separate saucepan to cook (about 15 minutes).
7. Lastly, add the sausages to the remaining broth and cook until done (about 20 minutes). Keep at a low boil to prevent bursting.
8. Cut meats, sausages and vegetables into large chunks. If desired, submerge again in boiling water just to heat through. Vegetables should be put in last.
9. Arrange the meat, sausages, vegetables and rice (this may also be served separately) on a large platter and serve.

Nutrition (per serving)
Calories 758
Carbs 72.9 g
Fat 28.9 g
Protein 49.8 g
Sodium 1326 mg

Pork Stew (Feijoada à Transmontana)

Serves: 8–10
Preparation Time: 10 minutes
Cooking Time: 2 hours 25 minutes

Ingredients
2 pounds riblets (back or spare ribs)
1 tablespoon sweet paprika
Salt, to taste
2 tablespoons olive oil
1 large onion, chopped
4 cloves garlic, minced
2 bay leaves
4 cups pork broth (or combination of broth and water)
2–3 pieces *chouriço*, sliced to bite size rounds
¼ cup tomato paste
1 28-ounce can diced tomatoes
2–4 pieces blood sausage, sliced to bite size rounds
2 15-ounce cans kidney beans, rinsed and drained
1 small cabbage, cut into bite size pieces

Directions
1. Place the riblets in a pot. Cover with water and bring to a boil.
2. Let simmer and cook until flesh is easy to cut through with a knife (about 1½ hours).
3. Remove the riblets and reserve the broth for later.
4. Season the riblets with salt and paprika and let sit to marinate.
5. Heat the oil in a skillet over medium and sauté the onion, garlic and bay leaf until onions are tender and translucent (about 5 minutes).
6. Add the broth and riblets and cook until flesh is tender (about 20 minutes).
7. Add the sausages, tomato paste, and diced tomatoes. Simmer for about 20 to 30 minutes.
8. Lastly, add the blood sausage, kidney beans and cabbage. Cook until cabbage is tender (about 10 minutes). Adjust saltiness, if needed and discard bay leaf.
9. Serve hot.

Nutrition (per serving)
Calories 623
Carbs 17.3 g
Fat 46.8 g
Protein 35.4 g
Sodium 762 mg

Beef Kebabs (*Estepadas*)

Serves: 8–10
Preparation Time: 15 minutes plus 4 hours marinating time
Cooking Time: 8–15 minutes

Ingredients
4 pounds beef sirloin, cut into cubes
2 onions, quartered
1 large bell pepper, cut into large cubes
4–5 small tomatoes, halved
1 tablespoon olive oil
Salt and pepper, to taste
3–4 tablespoons butter
Slices of thick, crusty bread (optional)

For marinade
8 cloves garlic, minced or pounded into a paste
4 bay leaves, crumbled
¾ cup Madeira or red wine of choice
3 tablespoons olive oil

Directions
1. Combine marinade ingredients and pour into a shallow dish or Ziploc bag.
2. Add the beef cubes and let marinate, refrigerated, for 4 hours to overnight.
3. Skewer the beef, alternating with onion, bell pepper and tomato. If using bamboo skewers, soak in water for 1 hour before using.
4. Brush with olive oil and season with salt and pepper.
5. Grill over a preheated grill (at medium heat) with an oiled grate. Cooking time depends on desired doneness (about 8 to 15 minutes).
6. Lay on slices of bread and brush with butter.
7. Serve.

Nutrition (per serving)
Calories 451
Carbs 5.1 g
Fat 19.6 g
Protein 55.4 g
Sodium 370 mg

Portuguese House Steak (*Bitoque*)

Serves: 4
Preparation Time: 15 minutes plus 2 hours marinating time
Cooking Time: 10 minutes

Ingredients
4 pieces sirloin steak, ½ inch thick
4 eggs
2–3 tablespoons oil for frying
Suggested sides: cooked rice, French fries and salad (see Portuguese Salad recipe p19)

For marinade
½ cup red or white wine
8 cloves garlic, minced
2 bay leaves
1 teaspoon paprika (optional)
2 tablespoons olive oil
Salt and pepper, to taste

Directions

1. Combine the ingredients for the marinade and place in a shallow container or Ziploc bag. Seal, refrigerate and let marinate for 2 hours to overnight.
2. Heat the oil in a skillet over medium heat.
3. Add the marinated steak and cook to sear. If steak seems dry, baste with a little marinade. Flip over when steak is browned and edges begin to crisp (about 4 minutes). Cook to desired doneness (about 2 to 4 minutes).
4. Transfer to serving dish.
5. Fry the eggs and place on top of the steaks.
6. Serve with side dishes of choice.

Nutrition (per serving)
Calories 602
Carbs 2.8 g
Fat 29 g
Protein 75.2 g
Sodium 529 mg

Veal Steak (Posta Mirandesa)

Serves: 4
Preparation Time: 15 minutes plus 2 hours marinating time
Cooking Time: 35 minutes (baking) / 4 minutes (grilling)

Ingredients
4 veal steaks (about 10½ ounces each), 1¼ inches thick
1 pound boiled potatoes
1 bunch boiled kale or collard greens
Salt and pepper, to taste
2–4 tablespoons butter (optional)
Chopped parsley for garnish

For marinade/sauce
6 cloves garlic, minced
1½ tablespoons chili sauce
⅓ cup white wine
⅓ cup olive oil
2 bay leaves
Salt, to taste

Directions
1. Combine the ingredients for the marinade. Add to the veal and let marinate, refrigerated, for 2 hours.
2. Preheat oven to 350°F.
3. Place the marinated veal in a baking dish.
4. Arrange the boiled potatoes around the veal.
5. Pour the marinade over the potatoes.
6. Bake until veal is of desired doneness and potatoes are slightly golden brown (about 35 minutes).
7. Dab with butter, if desired and garnish with chopped parsley.

Variation:
1. Season the veal with salt and pepper.
2. Grill over medium high heat to desired doneness (about 3–4 minutes per side).
3. Drizzle sauce over veal and vegetables.

Nutrition (per serving)
Calories 764
Carbs 59.9 g
Fat 25.7 g
Protein 68 g
Sodium 852 mg

Pork & Potatoes (*Rojões*)

Serves: 4
Preparation Time: 10 minutes plus 2 hours marinating time
Cooking Time: 45 minutes

Ingredients
2 pounds pork leg, cut into cubes
2 pounds potatoes, cut into bite size cubes
Salt and pepper, to taste
Oil for frying
2 bay leaves
Chopped parsley, for garnish

For marinade
⅔ cup white wine
4 cloves garlic, crushed
2 teaspoons paprika
2 teaspoons ground cumin
Salt and pepper, to taste

Directions
1. Mix the ingredients for the marinade together and marinate the pork for at least 2 hours to overnight.
2. Heat the oil in a skillet over medium heat.
3. Add the potatoes and sprinkle with salt and pepper.
4. Fry until golden brown. Remove from oil and drain on paper towels.
5. Pour out any oil in excess of 2 tablespoons from skillet.
6. Fry the marinated pork cubes until browned.
7. Pour the marinade over the pork and add the bay leaves.
8. Let simmer until the pork is tender (about 20 minutes), adding a little water if it gets too dry.
9. Add the potatoes and cook until heated through.
10. Sprinkle with chopped parsley.
11. Serve with rice.

Nutrition (per serving)
Calories 567
Carbs 37.3 g
Fat 20 g
Protein 51 g
Sodium 338 mg

Hunter-Style Rabbit Stew

Serves: 4
Preparation Time: 30 minutes
Cooking Time: 2 hours

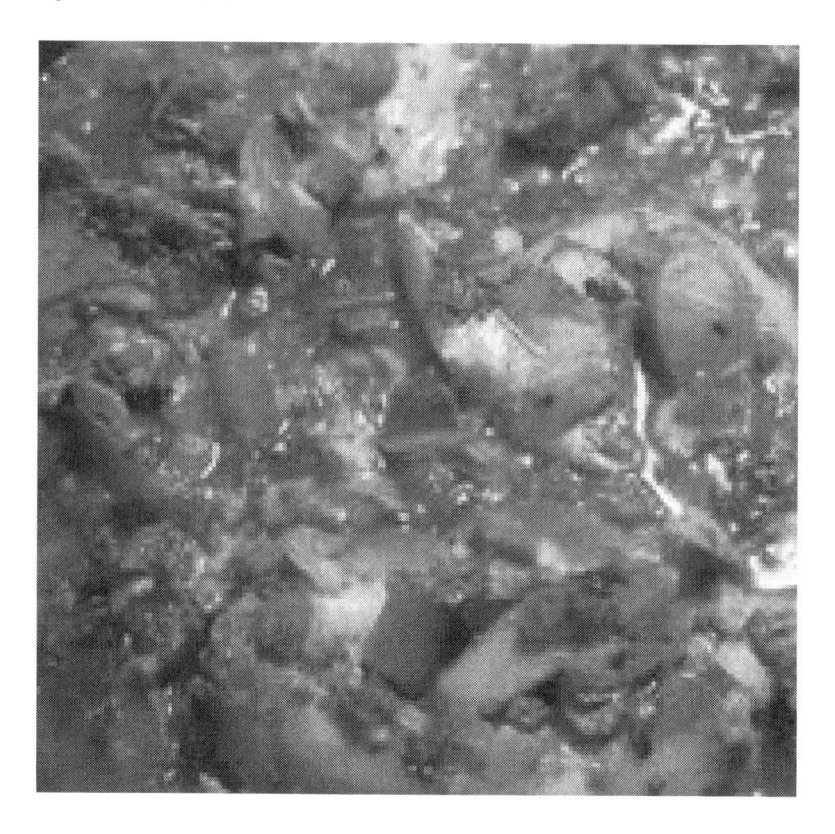

Ingredients
6 medium tomatoes
½ pound slab bacon, cut into cubes
3 pounds rabbit meat, cut into 8 pieces
Salt and pepper, to taste
Olive oil, if needed
3 onions, sliced
1 rabbit liver, finely chopped
3–4 cups mushrooms, sliced
4 garlic cloves, minced
1 cup dry red wine
2 bay leaves
1 tablespoon oregano leaves, chopped

1 tablespoon mint leaves, chopped
1 tablespoon parsley, for garnish

Directions

To peel the tomatoes
1. Wash the tomatoes and cut criss-cross slits at the ends.
2. Prepare a bowlful of ice water and a pot of boiling water.
3. Drop the tomatoes into the boiling water and remove after 30 seconds.
4. Place immediately in the ice water.
5. Remove after 5 minutes.
6. Peel the tomatoes, place in a bowl and set aside.

To prepare the stew
7. Heat a large skillet over medium high heat.
8. Add the bacon slices and cook until crisp (about 20 minutes). Remove from skillet and drain on paper towels.
9. Raise heat to medium high and add the rabbit slices. Season with salt and pepper.
10. Cook until evenly browned (about 15 minutes). Remove from skillet and let drain over paper towels.
11. Add a little oil, if needed, and the onions, liver and mushrooms. Sauté until browned (about 20 minutes).
12. Add the garlic and cook until fragrant (about 30 seconds).
13. Pour in the wine and let boil to deglaze. Scrap any brown bits from the bottom as wine boils.
14. Add the rabbit meat, tomatoes, bay leaves, oregano and mint. Press down on the tomatoes with a ladle or spatula to crush.
15. Let simmer until rabbit meat is done (about 1 hour).
16. Adjust flavor with salt and pepper, if needed.
17. If needed, remove meat and vegetables and continue cooking to reduce sauce. Pour sauce over meat and vegetables.
18. Sprinkle with parsley and serve with rice or bread.

Nutrition (per serving)
Calories 374
Carbs 13 g
Fat 27.7 g
Protein 9.6 g
Sodium 420 mg

Roast Suckling Pig (*Leitão*)

Serves: 20
Preparation Time: 30 minutes plus 4 hours marinating time
Cooking Time: 2 hours

Ingredients
1 10- to 15-pound suckling pig, washed and cleaned
2 bay leaves
1 cup white wine
1 tablespoon olive oil
2–3 oranges, sliced thinly

For rub
½ cup butter or lard, softened
2 teaspoons oregano
1 tablespoon parsley, finely chopped
Salt and pepper, to taste
4 cloves garlic, pounded into a paste

Directions
1. Combine the ingredients for the rub, pounding in a mortar and pestle if needed, to incorporate the seasonings well.
2. Dry the suckling pig as thoroughly as possible using a cloth or some paper towels.
3. Starting from the inside going out, spread the rub all over the pig, a little thicker inside than on the skin.
4. Place the bay leaves inside the pig.
5. Cover with plastic or foil and let marinate, refrigerated, for 4 hours.
6. Preheat oven to 250°F. Place a drip pan at the bottom (the drippings can be used as sauce to go with the meat later).
7. Remove the pig from the refrigerator and let warm to room temperature.
8. Drizzle with the wine and place stomach-down on the rack.
9. Bake until the internal temperature reaches 130°F (about 1½ hours). Every 20 to 30 minutes, baste with oil and change the pig's position. If the skin seems to be burning too quickly, cover loosely with foil.
10. Raise the oven temperature to 350 to 400°F and continue baking until the internal temperature reaches 155 to 160°F and the skin is crisp.
11. Transfer to a chopping board and let sit for about 15 minutes.
12. Serve whole or chopped, surrounded with orange wedges and with the collected drippings in a bowl as sauce.

Nutrition (per serving)
Calories 576
Carbs 0.5 g
Fat 33.9 g
Protein 62.8 g
Sodium 135 mg

Potatoes with Spicy Sausage (*Batatas Assadas Com Chouriço*)

Serves: 6
Preparation Time: 10 minutes
Cooking Time: 1 hour 30 minutes

Ingredients

1½–2 pounds *chouriço*, thinly sliced
2 pounds potatoes, scrubbed & cut into chunks
1 large onion, chopped
1 14-ounce can diced tomatoes
¼ cup parsley, chopped

For broth
3 cups chicken broth or water
3 tablespoons red wine vinegar
2 teaspoons sugar, or to taste
2½ tablespoons smoked paprika, or to taste
1 teaspoon hot sauce, or to taste
Salt and pepper, to taste

Directions

1. Preheat oven to 375°F.
2. Spread the sausage, potatoes, onion and tomatoes in a baking dish.
3. Whisk together the ingredients for the broth and pour over the sausage mixture.
4. Sprinkle with chopped parsley.
5. Bake until sausages and potatoes are done (about 1½ hours).

Nutrition (per serving)

Calories 487
Carbs 33.3 g
Fat 30.1 g
Protein 19.2 g
Sodium 92 mg

Linguiça, Chouriço and Parsley Omelet

Serves: 4
Preparation Time: 15 minutes
Cooking Time: 15 minutes

Ingredients
2–3 tablespoons olive oil, divided
1 piece *linguiça*, sliced into thin rounds
1 piece *chouriço*, removed from casing and sliced into thin rounds
6 eggs
¼ cup fresh parsley, finely chopped, plus some more for garnish
Salt and pepper, to taste

Directions
1. Heat about 1 tablespoon of the oil in a skillet.
2. Stir-fry the sausages until browned and crisp around the edges. Remove from skillet and drain on paper towels.
3. In a bowl, season the eggs with salt and pepper. Beat well.
4. Stir in sausages and chopped parsley.
5. Add the remaining oil in the skillet and heat over medium low heat. Pour egg mixture into the skillet.
6. Let cook until the omelet reaches desired doneness. Fold over if desired.
7. Sprinkle some more fresh parsley on top of the omelet, if desired. Serve with Portuguese Salad (recipe found in Salads category p19).

Nutrition (per serving)
Calories 229
Carbs 1.8 g
Fat 18.1 g
Protein 14.3 g
Sodium 182 mg

Pork Cutlets (*Bifanas*)

Serves: 4–6
Preparation Time: 10 minutes plus 2 hours marinating time
Cooking Time: 10 minutes

Ingredients
1½ pounds pork cutlets, boneless and sliced as thinly as possible
2 tablespoons olive oil, lard or bacon fat
4–6 crusty buns (optional)

For marinade
1 cup white wine or beer
¼ cup white wine vinegar
2 cloves garlic, minced
1 bay leaf, crumbled
1 teaspoon paprika paste (check Chicken Barbecue recipe p42)
1 teaspoon sweet or smoked paprika
¼ teaspoon *piri-piri* sauce

For sauce
¼ cup white wine or beer
½ cup beef broth (optional)
1 teaspoon paprika paste
¼ teaspoon smoked paprika
Salt and pepper, to taste

Directions
1. Combine the ingredients for the marinade and whisk well.
2. Pour into a Ziploc bag and add the pork cutlets.
3. Refrigerate and let marinate for 2 hours to overnight.
4. Remove the cutlets from the marinade, shaking off any excess. Let warm to room temperature.
5. Heat the oil in a skillet over medium heat.
6. Fry the cutlets in the oil until browned (about 1–2 minutes on each side, depending on thickness).
7. Add the sauce ingredients (including the beef broth, if you want moister bifanas) and bring to a boil.
8. Reduce heat and let cook for about 1–2 minutes, just enough for flavors to be absorbed by the pork.
9. To make sandwiches (optional), slit crusty buns, fill with cutlets and drizzle with sauce. Use mustard and piri-piri sauce as condiments.

Nutrition (per serving)
Calories 214
Carbs 1.8 g
Fat 6.9 g
Protein 25.6 g
Sodium 212 mg

Portuguese Roast Lamb

Serves: 4–6
Preparation Time: 20 minutes plus 2 hours marinating time
Cooking Time: 2 hours 10 minutes

Ingredients
2–3 pounds roast leg of lamb
1 medium onion, sliced thickly
4 strips of bacon
¾ cup red wine
1½ tablespoons tomato paste
2 bay leaves
1 tablespoon chopped parsley
1 pound potatoes (baby or cut into quarters), scrubbed
Salt and pepper, to taste
¼ cup margarine or butter

For marinade
1 medium onion, diced
4 cloves garlic, minced
¼ cup margarine or butter
1 teaspoon paprika
1 tablespoon fresh mint leaves, chopped
1 tablespoon *piri-piri* sauce (Piri-Piri Chicken recipe p47), or to taste
½ cup red wine
Salt and pepper, to taste
Herbs of your choice for garnish

Directions
1. Dry the lamb using paper towels and cut slits, about ¼ to ½ inch deep, on the surface.
2. Combine the ingredients for the marinade well and rub over the lamb.
3. Place in a container with a lid and refrigerate. Let marinate for 2 hours to overnight.
4. Preheat oven to 350°F.
5. Remove the marinated lamb from the refrigerator and allow it to warm up to room temperature.
6. Place the onion slices over the bottom of a baking dish and put the bacon strips on top.
7. Bake until the onions and bacon begin to brown at the edges (about 10 minutes).
8. Meanwhile, dissolve the tomato paste in the wine and add the bay leaves and parsley.
9. Place the lamb in baking dish over the bacon and onions.
10. Add the potatoes.
11. Pour the wine-tomato-paste mixture over the lamb and potatoes.
12. Season with salt and pepper, as needed, and pat with margarine or butter.
13. Bake until lamb is done: when internal temperature reaches 145 to 170°F or when it can be shredded easily with a fork (about 2 to 2½ hours). Scoop some of the sauce over the lamb and potatoes occasionally to prevent them from drying out.
14. Let sit for 15 minutes before serving. Sprinkle with herbs before serving.

Nutrition (per serving)
Calories 623
Carbs 18.9 g
Fat 26.7 g
Protein 68.7 g
Sodium 823 mg

Seafood

Monkfish with Tomatoes & Onion (*Tamboril com Tomate e Cebolas*)

Serves: 4
Preparation Time: 15 minutes plus 1 hour marinating time
Cooking Time: 35 minutes

Ingredients
3–4 monkfish fillets
3 tomatoes
½ cup flour
2–3 tablespoons olive oil
1 large onion, sliced into rings
½ cup white wine
⅛ teaspoon cinnamon
Handful of stuffed green olives, sliced

For seasoning
½ teaspoon oregano
Juice of 1 lemon
Salt and pepper, to taste

Directions
1. Peel the tomatoes (see instructions on how to peel tomatoes in Hunter-Style Rabbit Stew recipe p67) and chop. Set aside.
2. Pat the monkfish dry with paper towels.
3. Sprinkle with the seasoning ingredients and let marinate for 1 hour.
4. Shake off excess marinade and dredge the fillets with flour.
5. Heat the oil in a skillet over medium high heat.
6. Cook the fillets until browned on both sides (about 3–8 minutes).
7. Remove the fried fillets from the skillet and drain on paper towels.
8. Add more oil to the pan, if needed, and add the sliced onion.
9. Cook, with constant stirring, until onions are browned at the edges (about 5 minutes).
10. Add the tomatoes and wine.
11. Cover and simmer to soften the onions and tomatoes (about 20 minutes).
12. Add the cinnamon, salt and pepper.
13. Put the fish back into the skillet and simmer until it is cooked through and has absorbed the flavors (about 10 minutes).
14. Add olives and remove from heat.
15. Serve.

Nutrition (per serving)
Calories 221
Carbs 11.4 g
Fat 9.3 g
Protein 33.6 g
Sodium 183 mg

Seafood Stew (Cataplana de Marisco)

Serves: 6
Preparation Time: 10 minutes plus 20 minutes soaking
Cooking Time: 45 minutes

Ingredients
1 pound clams in the shell, scrubbed and rinsed
1 cup olive oil
3 pieces *chouriço*, removed from casing and sliced
2 medium onions, thinly sliced
4 garlic cloves, sliced
3 medium tomatoes, chopped
½ cup tomato sauce
2 tablespoons paprika paste (optional, find in Chicken Barbecue recipe p42)
1 bay leaf
½ cup white wine
1½ cups chicken or seafood broth
2 teaspoons paprika
A few pinches of chili flakes, to taste
Salt, to taste
1 pound mussels, scrubbed and rinsed
1 pound squid, cleaned and sliced

6 pieces sea bass fillet
2 tablespoons parsley, chopped
12 prawns, jumbo or extra-jumbo size
1 lemon, cut into wedges
Slices of crusty bread

Directions

1. Soak the clams in salty water for 20 minutes. Scoop out with a slotted spoon and discard the water (to prevent grits and sand from going back to clams, do not pour into a strainer). Set aside.
2. Heat the oil in a cataplana (check p6) over medium high heat. (A Dutch oven or wok with a good-fitting lid can also be used.)
3. Add the chouriço and fry until browned (5 minutes). Remove from the pan and set aside.
4. Add the onions and cook until translucent (about 3 minutes).
5. Add the garlic and cook until fragrant (about 1 minute).
6. Add the chopped tomatoes and cook, with stirring, until mushy (about 5 minutes).
7. Add the tomato sauce, paprika paste (optional) and bay leaf. Cover and reduce heat to low. Let simmer until sauce is reduced (about 8 minutes).
8. Stir in the wine, broth, paprika, chili flakes and salt.
9. Add the chouriço, mussels, clams and squid. Stir a bit.
10. Lay the fish fillet on top and sprinkle with chopped parsley.
11. Cover and let cook over high heat until the shellfish open (about 10 minutes).
12. Arrange the prawns and lemon wedges on top.
13. Cover and cook until the prawns have changed color and the fish is easy to flake (about 10 minutes).
14. Serve with slices of bread.

Nutrition (per serving)

Calories 625
Carbs 32.3 g
Fat 13.9 g
Protein 69.9 g
Sodium 1050 mg

Sautéed Cod (*Bacalhau à Brás*)

Serves: 2
Preparation Time: 15 minutes
Cooking Time: 35 minutes

Ingredients
2 fillets dehydrated *bacalhau* or salted cod
1 pound russet potatoes, peeled and shredded
Canola oil, for deep frying potatoes
3 tablespoons olive oil
4 cloves garlic, smashed
1 large onion, sliced very finely
3 or 4 eggs, beaten
1 teaspoon red chili flakes, or to taste
Salt and pepper, to taste
Black olives, for garnish
Chives, chopped, for garnish

Directions

1. Rehydrate the bacalhau (see how to rehydrate bacalhau in Bacalhau Salad recipe p23).
2. Pat the julienned potatoes dry with paper towels.
3. Heat the oil in a frying pan over high heat.
4. Fry the potatoes until golden brown. Drain over paper towels.
5. In another frying pan or skillet, heat the olive oil over medium high heat.
6. Add the garlic and onion and cook until the onion begins to brown at the edges (about 5 minutes).
7. Add the rehydrated bacalhau and cook over low heat until fish is done (about 15–20 minutes).
8. Transfer the fish to a plate and flake with forks.
9. Return the flaked fish to the hot skillet.
10. Add the beaten eggs and stir once or twice.
11. Before the eggs are fully cooked, add the fried potatoes.
12. Sprinkle with chili flakes and continue cooking while stirring to desired consistency (whether creamy or dry).
13. Adjust flavor with salt and pepper, according to taste.
14. Garnish with olives and chives.
15. Serve.

Nutrition (per serving)

Calories 477
Carbs 23 g
Fat 27 g
Protein 30 g
Sodium 290 mg

Octopus in Garlic & Olive Oil (*Polvo à Lagareiro*)

Serves: 4
Preparation Time: 5 minutes
Cooking Time: 1 hour

Ingredients
1 or 2 pieces whole octopus (about 3 pounds), washed and cleaned
1 large onion, whole, peeled
2 pounds baby potatoes, scrubbed and washed
Salt, to taste
4 bay leaves
1 bunch of parsley, chopped
6 cloves garlic, crushed
1½ teaspoons balsamic vinegar
3 cups olive oil (or more, to cover octopus)

Directions
1. Preheat oven to 400°F.
2. Place the octopus in a pressure cooker with the (unsliced) onion and pressure cook for 15 minutes. Remove from the pot and transfer to a non-reactive baking dish.
3. Place the potatoes in another baking dish and sprinkle with salt. Drizzle with olive oil.
4. Sprinkle the garlic, bay leaves, parsley and vinegar over the octopus.
5. Pour enough olive oil to almost cover the octopus.
6. Bake both the octopus and potatoes until tender (about 15–20 minutes), ladling the oil over the octopus occasionally to prevent drying.
7. Remove from oven.
8. Cut the octopus into large pieces and mix with the potatoes.
9. Arrange on a serving platter and drizzle with the hot olive oil sauce.

Nutrition (per serving)
Calories 733
Carbs 50.5 g
Fat 38.5 g
Protein 48 g
Sodium 58 mg

Charcoal-Grilled Squid (*Lulas Grelhadas*)

Serves: 4–6
Preparation Time: 20 minutes
Cooking Time: 6 minutes

Ingredients
2 pounds squid, cleaned
Chopped parsley, for garnish
1 lemon, sliced

For marinade
1 cup olive oil
4 cloves garlic, pounded into a paste
Salt and pepper, to taste
1 tablespoon chopped fresh sage

Directions
1. Combine the ingredients for the marinade and place in a dish.
2. Wipe the squid dry, as thoroughly as possible, with paper towels.
3. Marinate the squid for 20 minutes.
4. Preheat the grill to high heat (hot coals are ideal) and oil the grate.
5. Sear the squid to brown quickly (about 3 minutes on each side). Overcooking will make the squid rubbery.
6. Sprinkle with parsley and serve with lemon slices.

Nutrition (per serving)
Calories 243
Carbs 1 g
Fat 27 g
Protein 0.2 g
Sodium 570 mg

Fish Stew (Caldeirada de Peixe)

Serves: 4
Preparation Time: 20 minutes
Cooking Time: 45 minutes

Ingredients
4 large, meaty fish (such as sea bass, cod, sea bream, red snapper or rehydrated *bacalhau* for which you can find instructions in Bacalhau Salad recipe p23), cleaned and in large cuts
¼ cup extra-virgin olive oil
1 large onion, sliced thinly
4 cloves garlic, minced
3 large tomatoes, sliced
2 medium red or green (or combination) bell peppers, cut into bite size pieces
4 large potatoes, cubed
2 bay leaves
½ cup cilantro, chopped
1 tablespoon paprika
Sea salt, to taste
1½ cups white wine

Directions
1. Prepare a large pot with a lid.
2. Take roughly a third of each ingredient and layer them in this order: olive oil, onion, garlic, tomato, bell pepper, potatoes, bay leaf, cilantro, paprika and salt. Repeat until the ingredients are used up.
3. Pour in the white wine.
4. Place the lid and cook over low heat until the fish and potatoes are done (about 45–60 minutes, depending on the thickness).
5. Typically served with crusty bread, olives and white wine.

Nutrition (per serving)
Calories 732
Carbs 72.1 g
Fat 16.7 g
Protein 59.2 g
Sodium 540 mg

Charcoal-Grilled Sardines (*Sardinhas Assadas*)

Serves: 4–6
Preparation Time: 10 minutes plus 1 hour marinating time
Cooking Time: 3–4 minutes

Ingredients
16 pieces medium fresh sardines, cleaned, scaled and rinsed
Salt, to taste
⅓ cup olive oil
Chopped parsley, for garnish

Directions
1. Pat the sardines dry with paper towels.
2. Sprinkle liberally with salt and place in a colander. Let stand for 1 hour (this helps make the flesh firmer).
3. Preheat a grill and grease the grate.
4. Dry the salted sardines with paper towels and brush with the olive oil.
5. Grill for about 3–4 minutes per side.
6. Drizzle with a little more olive oil and season with salt, if needed.
7. Sprinkle with chopped parsley and serve. Goes well with cornbread (find recipe in Sides category p105) and a salad.

Nutrition (per serving)
Calories 292
Carbs 7.6 g
Fat 35.3 g
Protein 35.3 g
Sodium 707 mg

Codfish Croquettes (*Pasteis de Bacalhau*)

Serves: 20
Preparation Time: 20 minutes
Cooking Time: 50 minutes

Ingredients
1 pound boneless *bacalhau*
2 cups milk
4 potatoes, scrubbed
2 cloves garlic, pounded to a paste
1 medium onion, minced
2 tablespoons cilantro or parsley (or combination thereof), chopped
2 eggs, slightly beaten
Salt and pepper, to taste
Oil for frying
1 lemon, sliced (optional)

Directions
1. Rehydrate the bacalhau (see instructions in Bacalhau Salad recipe p23).
2. Place the rehydrated bacalhau in a pot or saucepan and pour in the milk. If needed, add water to cover by 1 inch.
3. Bring to a boil and gently simmer until fish is tender (about 20 minutes).
4. Drain and rinse well.
5. While simmering the bacalhau, place the potatoes in a pot, cover with water and boil until tender (about 20 minutes). Drain and peel.
6. Flake the fish and add the peeled potatoes. Mash well together. Let cool.
7. When cooled, add the garlic, onion, cilantro and/or parsley, and eggs. Mix together well and season with salt and pepper to taste.
8. Scoop out a spoonful. To shape, use 2 spoons and scrape the mixture from one spoon to another once or twice to make oval-shaped. Drop this in preheated oil in a skillet. Keep shaping additional spoonfuls and dropping them into the oil until the mixture is used up.
9. Deep fry until golden brown and then drain on paper towels.
10. Serve with lemon slices (optional).

Nutrition (per serving)
Calories 63
Carbs 9 g
Fat 2 g
Protein 5 g
Sodium 315 mg

Sides

Tomato Rice (*Arroz de Tomate*)

Serves: 4
Preparation Time: 10 minutes
Cooking Time: 30 minutes

Ingredients
2 tablespoons olive oil
1 tablespoon bacon fat or margarine
1 medium onion, chopped
4 cloves garlic, minced
2 large tomatoes, chopped
1 bay leaf
Red pepper flakes, to taste
1½ cups meat or vegetable broth

1 cup short-grain white rice
3 tablespoons chopped cilantro or parsley (or combination)
Salt and pepper, to taste

Directions
1. Heat the oil in a pot over medium high heat. (If cooking everything in the pot and not in a rice cooker, make sure the pot has a well-fitted lid.)
2. Melt the bacon fat or margarine in the oil.
3. Sauté the onions and garlic until fragrant (about 2 minutes).
4. Add the tomatoes, bay leaf and red pepper flakes. Cook, with stirring, until the tomatoes are softened and almost mushy (about 5 minutes).
5. Add the broth. The mixture may be transferred to a rice cooker at this point.
6. Stir in the rice, salt and pepper.
7. Cover and let cook.
8. As soon as the mixture starts to boil, add the cilantro and/or parsley
9. Replace the cover. If cooking in a pot, reduce heat and let simmer until liquid is absorbed and rice is tender or of desired consistency (about 20 minutes; it can be porridge-like or drier). If using a rice cooker, just wait for it to switch off automatically.
10. Turn off heat but let sit for 10 minutes before removing lid.
11. Goes well with meat and fish.

Nutrition (per serving)
Calories 216
Carbs 28.1 g
Fat 10.4 g
Protein 3.4 g
Sodium 478 mg

Corn Bread (*Broa de Milho*)

Serves: 12–24
Preparation Time: 40 minutes plus 2¼ hours proofing time
Cooking Time: 25 minutes

Ingredients
2 cups yellow cornmeal plus extra for dusting
1½ cups hot water
1 cup milk, warmed
4 teaspoons instant yeast
5 cups all-purpose flour plus extra for dusting
1 tablespoon salt
¼ cup honey
2 tablespoons olive oil plus extra for greasing

Directions
1. Place the cornmeal in a bowl and stir in the hot water.
2. Add the milk and mix. Let sit until lukewarm (about 15 minutes).
3. Knead in the rest of the ingredients to make a slightly sticky dough.
4. Lightly grease two bowls.
5. Divide the dough and place it into the bowls.
6. Flip the dough over in the bowl and cover with a dish towel.
7. Let rise until puffy (1½ hours).
8. Prepare a greased baking sheet and dust with cornmeal. Set aside.
9. Place the expanded dough on a floured surface.
10. Knead very briefly and form into a ball. Do the same for the other piece.
11. Place the dough onto the prepared baking sheet.
12. Cover and let rise again until puffy (45 minutes).
13. Preheat oven to 450°F.
14. When the dough is ready, spritz the surface lightly with water.
15. Make four ¼-inch slashes on top.
16. Bake for 10 minutes, then reduce oven temperature to 400°F.
17. Continue baking until golden brown (about 15 minutes).
18. Let set for 15 minutes before slicing.
19. Slice and serve. Traditionally eaten for breakfast or as an accompaniment for other dishes (like Caldo Verde, recipe in Soups category p29, and Eggs with Peas & Linguiça, recipe found in Poultry category p45).

Nutrition (per serving)
Calories 148
Carbs 27 g
Fat 2 g
Protein 4 g
Sodium 276 mg

Pan-Fried Crumbs with Kale & Black-Eyed Beans (*Migas*)

Serves: 4–6
Preparation Time: 5 minutes
Cooking Time: 10 minutes

Ingredients
1 bunch kale leaves, shredded
1 15½-ounce can black-eyed peas
½ **Portuguese corn bread** (recipe in Sides category p105), crumbled
2 garlic cloves, smashed
Handful of roasted pine nuts (optional)
¼ cup olive oil
Salt and pepper, to taste
Advertisements

Directions

1. Blanch the black-eyed peas (this should be very quick or else they will become mushy). Drain and set aside.
2. Boil a fresh batch of water and sprinkle with salt. Boil the kale until tender (about 8 minutes). Remove with a slotted spoon onto a colander. Cool down under tap water and drain well. Pat dry with paper towels, if needed.
3. Heat the oil in a skillet over medium heat.
4. Add the garlic and cook until browned (about 2 minutes). Discard the garlic.
5. Add the bread crumbs and season with salt and pepper. Cook, with stirring, until golden brown.
6. Add the kale, black-eyed peas and pine nuts (if using). Cook just to heat through (about 30 seconds).
7. Serve while hot. Goes well with meat and fish dishes.

Nutrition (per serving)
Calories 262
Carbs 33.8 g
Fat 12.8 g
Protein 4.8 g
Sodium 219 mg

Portuguese Rice with Beans

Serves: 8
Preparation Time: 5 minutes
Cooking Time: 20–25 minutes

Ingredients
¼ cup olive oil
1 medium onion, finely chopped
2 tablespoons fresh parsley, finely chopped
2-4 teaspoons paprika, to taste
2 bay leaves
3 cups meat or vegetable broth
3 cups water
3 cups long grain rice, uncooked
Salt and pepper, to taste
1 15-ounce can kidney beans, rinsed well and drained

Directions

1. Heat the oil in a large saucepan over medium-high heat.
2. Sauté the onions until slightly browned (about 3 minutes).
3. Add the parsley, paprika and bay leaves and cook until fragrant (about 1 minute).
4. Add the broth and water. The mixture may be transferred to a rice cooker at this point.
5. Stir in the rice.
6. Season with salt and pepper, then cover and let cook.
7. As soon as the mixture starts to boil, add the kidney beans and replace the cover.
8. Reduce heat and let simmer until liquid is absorbed and rice is tender (about 20 minutes), or until the rice cooker shuts off automatically.
9. Turn off heat but let sit for 10 minutes before removing lid.
10. Fluff rice and serve.

Nutrition (per serving)

Calories 322
Carbs 57.7 g
Fat 7.3 g
Protein 5.2 g
Sodium 592 mg

Poor Man's Stew (*Açorda*)

Serves: 2
Preparation Time: 10 minutes
Cooking Time: 25 minutes

Ingredients
2 thick slices bread (at least two days old), toasted and torn into large pieces
2 eggs
Salt and pepper, to taste
Flavor paste
Broth

For broth
3 cups chicken or vegetable broth
4 garlic cloves, peeled
1 sprig fresh cilantro or parsley
1 tablespoon olive oil

For flavor paste
1 garlic clove, peeled and pounded into a paste
Salt and pepper to taste
¼ cup fresh cilantro or parsley (or combination), finely chopped
1½ tablespoons olive oil

Directions
For broth
1. In a pot, bring the chicken or vegetable broth to a boil.
2. Add the rest of the broth ingredients.
3. Reduce heat and gently simmer for 20 minutes. Prepare the flavor paste while the broth is simmering.

For flavor paste
4. In a mortar and pestle, pound the garlic with salt and pepper.
5. Add the cilantro and/or parsley.
6. Add the olive oil gradually, while pounding, until a paste is formed. Transfer to a serving dish.

To make the creamy stew
7. Place the toasted bread over the flavor paste in the serving dish.
8. Using a slotted spoon, remove the garlic and cilantro from the broth.
9. Break the eggs and drop them into the simmering broth to poach (about 3 minutes).
10. Remove the poached eggs from the broth with a slotted spoon and place on top of the bread.
11. Season the broth with salt and pepper to taste and ladle over the eggs while hot.
12. Serve.

Nutrition (per serving)
Calories 330
Carbs 18.9 g
Fat 24.3 g
Protein 11.5 g
Sodium 1089 mg

Desserts

Golden Slices (*Fatias Douradas*)

Serves: 4–8
Preparation Time: 10 minutes
Cooking Time: 8–10 minutes

Ingredients
8–12 thick slices of bread (at least a day old)
4–6 eggs, beaten well
Milk mixture
Cooking oil for frying
Sugar for dusting
Honey (optional)

For milk mixture
1½ cups milk
1 tablespoon flour

1 teaspoon cinnamon powder
Dash of nutmeg (optional)

For dusting
½ cup powdered sugar or 1 cup refined sugar
2 teaspoons cinnamon powder, or to taste

Directions
1. Combine ingredients for dusting and put in a shallow dish.
2. Whisk together the milk, flour, cinnamon and nutmeg (if using) and pour into a shallow bowl.
3. Heat up the oil for frying, about 1 inch deep, over high heat. (With a non-stick pan, less oil will be needed.)
4. Taking one slice of bread at a time, dip into milk mixture until evenly absorbed. Tap out excess.
5. Next, dip into the beaten eggs. Coat well and tap out excess.
6. Place in hot oil to fry.
7. While the first slice is being fried, repeat the dipping steps with the next slice of bread and so on up to the last slice.
8. Fry until golden, flipping the slices over for even browning.
9. Drain on paper towels and let cool slightly.
10. Dip the fried slices in the sugar-cinnamon mixture and coat well, or if using powdered sugar, simply sift the mixture over the fried slices. Drizzle with honey, if desired.
11. Serve.

Nutrition *(per serving)*
Calories 326
Carbs 54.2 g
Fat 7.4 g
Protein 10.6 g
Sodium 339 mg

Portuguese Doughnuts (*Malassadas*)

Serves: 30–40
Preparation Time: 30 minutes plus 2 hours fermentation
Cooking Time: 2–3 minutes

Ingredients
1 packet of yeast
¾ cup warm water, divided
2½ pounds baking flour
1½ teaspoons salt
6 eggs, at room temperature
4 tablespoons sugar, divided
1 cup butter
2 tablespoons vegetable shortening
¾ cup milk
¾ cup water
Oil for frying
Sugar for dusting

Directions
1. Dissolve the yeast and 1 teaspoon of the sugar in ¼ cup of the warm water; set aside.
2. In a small bowl, beat the eggs with 1 tablespoon sugar until thick.
3. Melt the butter and then add the shortening, milk, and remaining warm water. Let cool slightly.
4. Pour in the egg yolks while mixing.
5. In a very large bowl, mix the flour and salt.
6. Pour in the egg yolk mixture.
7. Mix with your hands.
8. Add half of the water and mix, using a folding motion from the sides to the center. Repeat a few times.
9. Add the yeast mixture and continue kneading.
10. Add more water gradually, making the dough a bit wet and sticky. (Water helps develop the gluten.)
11. Continue kneading until the dough starts to hold together.
12. Pull out a piece about the size of an egg and see if it can be stretched thin without breaking. The dough is not ready if it breaks. Continue kneading and adding water gradually until this is achieved. The dough will not be dry and smooth like bread dough.
13. When the dough is ready, push sides inward to make it ball-shaped and sprinkle with flour.
14. Cover with a kitchen cloth or towel and leave for 2 hours to expand.
15. Heat oil in a pan over high heat, about 2–3 inches deep.
16. Pull out a handful of dough and stretch to about the size of a slice of bread. The middle part should be thin and stretched out (with no tearing) while the edges should be slightly thicker.
17. Fry, flipping over once, until the edges are golden brown (2–3 minutes).The centers will be lighter in color
18. Drain over paper towels and let cool slightly.
19. Dip in a bowl of sugar or shake in a bag to coat.
20. Serve warm.

*The malassadas become tough in a day or two. Fry all the dough, let cool completely and put in airtight containers. Keep frozen. Reheat for a few seconds in the microwave and then coat with sugar.

Nutrition (per serving)
Calories 125
Carbs 13.7 g
Fat 7 g
Protein 2 g
Sodium 106 mg

Old-Fashioned Sweet Rice Pudding (*Arroz Doce*)

Serves: 4–6
Preparation Time: 15 minutes
Cooking Time: 50–55 minutes

Ingredients
2 cups water
¼ teaspoon salt
1 cup Arborio rice (Italian sticky rice), uncooked
1 stick cinnamon
Rind of 1 lemon, in large pieces
¼ cup butter, divided
4¼ cups whole milk and about ¼ extra for egg yolks (if using)
3–4 egg yolks, beaten (optional)
Vanilla (optional)

Directions

1. In a saucepan, combine the water and salt.
2. Bring to a boil and then stir in the rice.
3. Reduce heat to medium low and simmer, stirring continuously, until the rice has absorbed almost all the water (about 20 minutes). Do not let it dry up completely so as not to burn it.
4. Add the cinnamon, lemon rind, half the butter and the milk. Adjust heat to medium high.
5. With continuous stirring, bring to a boil again and then reduce to a simmer. Check for any rice that may have stuck to the bottom of the pan. Cook 20 minutes.
6. Add the remaining butter and continue stirring while simmering for 10 more minutes.
7. If using egg yolks (for a richer pudding), beat them well in a small bowl with the extra milk. Pour this into the mixture gradually, mixing well after each addition. Cook a little longer to cook the yolks and thicken the mixture further.
8. Stir in vanilla (optional).
9. Remove from heat.
10. Discard the cinnamon stick and lemon rind.
11. Pour into serving containers and sprinkle with cinnamon.
12. May be served chilled or at room temperature.

Nutrition (per serving)

Calories 392
Carbs 78.4 g
Fat 6.8 g
Protein 5.5 g
Sodium 86 mg

Chocolate 'Salami' (*Salame de Chocolate*)

Serves: 16–20
Preparation Time: 10 minutes plus 4 hours refrigeration
Cooking Time: 5 minutes

Ingredients
2 7-ounce packs Marie biscuits
1 cup butter or margarine
1 cup sugar, divided
1¾ cups cocoa powder
3 egg yolks, slightly beaten
2 tablespoons port wine (optional)

Directions
1. Beat the biscuits in a bag to break them into coarse pieces (or just use your hands to break each into four). Set aside.
2. In a medium heat-proof bowl, whisk 2 tablespoons sugar with the egg yolks. Set aside.
3. Place the butter, cocoa and remaining sugar in a heavy bottomed pan over medium to low heat. Whisk continuously until the sugar is dissolved and the mixture is smooth and glossy.
4. Remove from heat and gradually pour into the egg yolks, whisking well after each addition.
5. Whisk in the port, if using.
6. Pour over biscuits and mix to coat evenly. Let cool to room temperature.
7. If the mixture is too soft, refrigerate for about 15 minutes or until thick enough to mold.
8. Cut a length of aluminum foil or plastic wrap (about 1½ feet).
9. Put half of the mixture at the center and even it out sideways with a spatula.
10. Fold the foil/wrap over and roll to shape into a log or sausage shape.
11. Twist the ends to seal.
12. Repeat with the remaining mixture.
13. Refrigerate for 4 hours to overnight, or until firm enough to slice.
14. Remove the foil/wrap and roll in confectioners' sugar to make it look like real salami. Tie with string, if desired, for a more salami-like presentation.
15. Slice and serve.

Nutrition (per serving)
Calories 233
Carbs 28.8 g
Fat 12.9 g
Protein 3.7 g
Sodium 72 mg

Custard Tarts (*Pasteis de Nata*)

Serves: 12
Preparation Time: 45 minutes plus 1 hour refrigeration time
Cooking Time: 20 minutes

Ingredients
For pastry shell
2 cups all-purpose flour, plus more for dusting
½ teaspoon baking powder
½ teaspoon salt
¾ cup unsalted butter, cut into cubes
⅔ cup ice water

For custard filling
1 tablespoon cornstarch
1½ cups heavy cream
1½ teaspoons vanilla
1 cup granulated sugar
Rind of 1 lemon, large pieces
6 egg yolks
1 stick cinnamon

For garnish
⅓ cup confectioners' sugar
1 teaspoon cinnamon

Directions

For pastry shell
1. Mix the flour, baking powder and salt.
2. Add in the butter, and using your hands or a mixer with dough hook attachment, mix or pulse in small spurts until the mixture looks like coarse cornmeal.
3. While mixing, pour in half of the water in a stream. Add the rest of the water by the tablespoonful, scraping down the sides of the bowl when needed, until the mixture begins to hold together.
4. Press the dough together to form a ball.
5. Line your work surface with plastic wrap.
6. Place the ball of dough at the center of the plastic and flatten it with your hands to form a thick disc.
7. Wrap the dough and refrigerate for 1 hour.
8. When the dough is ready to be rolled out, preheat oven to 350°F.
9. Divide the dough in half and gently compress each portion into a ball.
10. Dust the work surface with flour and roll out the dough thinly (to about 1/16 of an inch).
11. Use a cutter or wide-mouthed glass or jar to cut out 4-inch circles.
12. Press the circles into muffin molds and trim away the excess with a knife.
13. Repeat with the other half of the dough until you have filled 12 muffin molds.
14. Place cupcake liners over the pastry and fill with pastry weights or beans.
15. Bake for 10 minutes.

For the filling
16. Mix the ingredients together in a heavy-bottomed pan.
17. Bring to a boil with stirring. Immediately remove from heat and let cool (about 10 minutes).
18. Remove the cinnamon stick and lemon rind and fill the pastry shells.
19. Bake until the filling swells and dark brown spots form on the surface (about 20 minutes).
20. Place on a rack to cool for about 15 minutes. Centers may still be jiggly but will set during cooling.
21. Sift the sugar-cinnamon garnish over the pastries.
22. Serve warm.

Variation: Use store-bought puff pastry. Unfold and cut into circles. Press into greased muffin cups and trim off excess. Fill with the custard mixture and bake at 350–400°F for 20–25 minutes (or according to packaging instructions).

Nutrition (per serving)
Calories 363
Carbs 36.4 g
Fat 22.8 g
Protein 4.1 g
Sodium 212 mg

Recipe Index

Appetizers & Snacks _____7
   Clams in Lemon & Garlic (Ameijoas à Bulhão Pato) ____7
   Stone-Baked Bread (Bolo do Caco)_____9
   Salted Lupini Beans (Tremoços) _____11
   Shrimp Croquettes (Rissóis de Camarão) _____13
Salads _____15
   Portuguese Salad _____15
   Portuguese Potato Salad _____17
   Bacalhau Salad (Salada de Bacalhau)_____19
   Octopus Salad (Salada de Polvo) _____21
   Tomato Salad (Salada de Tomate)_____23
Soups_____25
   Portuguese Green Soup (Caldo Verde)_____25
   Cabbage & Bean Soup (Sopa de Couve Repolho com
   Feijão Branco) _____27
   Kale Soup (Sopa de Couves) _____29
   Stone Soup (Sopa de Piedra)_____31
Poultry _____33
   Garlic Chicken (Frango Com Alho) _____33
   Duck Rice (Arroz de Pato) _____35
   Chicken Barbecue (Frango No Churrasco)_____38
   Eggs with Peas & Linguiça_____41
   Piri-Piri Chicken_____43
Pork, Beef & Lamb _____45
   Hearty Meat Sandwich with Beer Sauce (Francesinha)__45
   Portuguese Cozido (Cozido à Portuguesa) _____47
   Pork Stew (Feijoada à Transmontana) _____49
   Beef Kebabs (Estepadas) _____51
   Portuguese House Steak (Bitoque) _____53
   Veal Steak (Posta Mirandesa) _____55
   Pork & Potatoes (Rojões) _____57
   Hunter-Style Rabbit Stew _____59

Roast Suckling Pig (Leitão) _____ 61
Potatoes with Spicy Sausage (Batatas Assadas Com Chouriço) _____ 63
Linguiça, Chouriço and Parsley Omelet _____ 65
Pork Cutlets (Bifanas) _____ 67
Portuguese Roast Lamb _____ 69

Seafood _____ 71
Monkfish with Tomatoes & Onion (Tamboril com Tomate e Cebolas) _____ 71
Seafood Stew (Cataplana de Marisco) _____ 73
Sautéed Cod (Bacalhau à Brás) _____ 75
Octopus in Garlic & Olive Oil (Polvo à Lagareiro) _____ 77
Charcoal-Grilled Squid (Lulas Grelhadas) _____ 79
Fish Stew (Caldeirada de Peixe) _____ 81
Charcoal-Grilled Sardines (Sardinhas Assadas) _____ 83
Codfish Croquettes (Pasteis de Bacalhau) _____ 85

Sides _____ 87
Tomato Rice (Arroz de Tomate) _____ 87
Corn Bread (Broa de Milho) _____ 89
Pan-Fried Crumbs with Kale & Black-Eyed Beans (Migas) _____ 91
Portuguese Rice with Beans _____ 93
Poor Man's Stew (Açorda) _____ 95

Desserts _____ 97
Golden Slices (Fatias Douradas) _____ 97
Portuguese Doughnuts (Malassadas) _____ 99
Old-Fashioned Sweet Rice Pudding (Arroz Doce) _____ 101
Chocolate 'Salami' (Salame de Chocolate) _____ 103
Custard Tarts (Pasteis de Nata) _____ 105

Image Credits

Cataplana

By Sevinha (Own work) [Public domain], via Wikimedia Commons

Portuguese Codizo

By Adriao (Own work) [CC BY 3.0 (http://creativecommons.org/licenses/by/3.0) or GFDL (http://www.gnu.org/copyleft/fdl.html)], via Wikimedia Commons

Veal Steak (Posta Mirandesa)

https://www.tripadvisor.com/LocationPhotoDirectLink-g189171-d8361113-i164222494-Recanto_Dos_Amigos-Braga_Braga_District_Northern_Portugal.html#164222494

This photo of Recanto Dos Amigos is courtesy of TripAdvisor

Bifano sandwich

By Alberto González [CC BY-SA 3.0 (http://creativecommons.org/licenses/by-sa/3.0)], via Wikimedia Commons

Also by Sarah Spencer

Shown below are some of Sarah's other books.

TOTALLY
MEXICAN
CLASSIC AND AUTHENTIC RECIPES FROM MEXICO
SARAH SPENCER

French
BISTRO
COOKING
Sarah Spencer

TOTALLY
VIETNAMESE
CLASSIC VIETNAMESE RECIPES TO MAKE AT HOME
SARAH SPENCER

TOTALLY
KOREAN
CLASSIC KOREAN RECIPES TO MAKE AT HOME
SARAH SPENCER

LOUISIANA
COOKING
EASY CAJUN AND CREOLE
RECIPES FROM LOUISIANA
SARAH SPENCER

BEST BACKYARD
BBQ RECIPES
From Around the World
100 QUICK AND EASY
GRILLING RECIPES
SARAH SPENCER

Appendix - Cooking Conversion Charts

1. Measuring Equivalent Chart

Type	Imperial	Imperial	Metric
Weight	1 dry ounce		28g
	1 pound	16 dry ounces	0.45 kg
Volume	1 teaspoon		5 ml
	1 dessert spoon	2 teaspoons	10 ml
	1 tablespoon	3 teaspoons	15 ml
	1 Australian tablespoon	4 teaspoons	20 ml
	1 fluid ounce	2 tablespoons	30 ml
	1 cup	16 tablespoons	240 ml
	1 cup	8 fluid ounces	240 ml
	1 pint	2 cups	470 ml
	1 quart	2 pints	0.95 l
	1 gallon	4 quarts	3.8 l
Length	1 inch		2.54 cm

* Numbers are rounded to the closest equivalent

2. Oven Temperature Equivalent Chart

T(°F)	T(°C)
220	100
225	110
250	120
275	140
300	150
325	160
350	180
375	190
400	200
425	220
450	230
475	250
500	260

* T(°C) = [T(°F)-32] * 5/9
** T(°F) = T(°C) * 9/5 + 32
*** Numbers are rounded to the closest equivalent